Schizophrenia

Psychotherapy Treatment for Mental Illness

Don't Give Up on Your Loved One

Jame Stafford

Disclaimer

This document is geared towards providing exact and reliable information in regards to the topic and issue covered. The publication is sold with the idea that the publisher is not required to render accounting, officially permitted, or otherwise, qualified services. If advice is necessary, legal or professional, a practiced individual in the profession should be ordered. In no way is it legal to reproduce, duplicate, or transmit any part of this document in either electronic means or in printed format. Recording of this publication is strictly prohibited and any storage of this document is not allowed unless with written permission from the publisher. All rights reserved. The information provided herein is stated to be truthful and consistent, in that any liability, in terms of inattention or otherwise, by any usage or abuse of any policies, processes, or directions contained within is the solitary and utter responsibility of the recipient reader. Under no circumstances will any legal responsibility or blame be held against the publisher for any reparation, damages, or monetary loss due to the information herein, either directly or indirectly. The information herein is offered for informational purposes solely, and is universal as so. The presentation of the information is without contract or any type of guarantee assurance. This book is not intended for use as a source of legal, medical, business, accounting or financial advice. All readers are advised to seek services of competent professionals in the legal, medical, business, accounting, and finance fields.

Table of Contents

12. Computer-Based Therapy Can Help Treat Patients of Schizophrenia

Introduction

Schizophrenia happens to be one of the most rampant mental disorders, and is usually characterized by an altered mental outlook towards reality. It is one of the most common mental illnesses that affect people in many parts of the world. The disorder is normally associated with breakdown of thoughts and being emotionally irresponsible. In many cases, an individual suffering from schizophrenia has delusions, hallucinations, paranoia and may become dysfunctional. Schizophrenia is believed to be as a result of genetic, psychological, social, neurological and environmental factors. It requires lifelong treatment even when symptoms have subsided. With proper medication and psycho social therapy, you can manage this terrible condition.

Chapter I

What Is Schizophrenia?

Schizophrenia is an incredible example of mental muddle which is exemplified by crumbling of thought processes and emotional receptiveness.

It can be straightforwardly acknowledged by auditory hallucinations, paranoid or bizarre illusions, dislocated speech or thinking aptitude pursued by social or occupational dysfunction.

The warning signs initiate untimely in the adulthood. The disease is recognized to affect about 1% of the human population with about 2 million patients from the United States unaided.

Schizophrenia is also known as split personality disorder and it affects men extra recurrently in contrast to women.

A number of aspects play decisive task in aggravating the symptoms of this disorder and these issues are genetic parameters, early environment, neurobiology, physiological and social processes. Some drugs also contribute a petite portion in making the condition of the patient poorer.

In the present scenario researchers are very much spotlighted on the neurobiological factors but no apposite consequence has cropped up.

The authentic cause of the disorder is still a contentious concern and the intact argument is centered on the verity that whether the disorder is due to a single cause or other syndromes are also correlated with it.

The word schizophrenia has been taken from a Greek word implicating split mind. Antipsychotic medication is usually applied while treating the patients of this disorder as it curbs dopamine and serotonin receptor bustle.

Psychotherapy tracked by social and vocational rehabilitation play an imperative role in treatment. In very ruthless cases hospitalization becomes obligatory.

The disorder is essentially branded to influence cognition causing setbacks connected with behavior and emotions. Patients also suffer from depression and anxiety disorders. The typical life span of the patient is of 12-15 years after the identification of the disease.

Schizophrenia occurs in stages that continue advancing if no medical measures are taken. However it is worth noting that the disorder is more severe if it developed during the young age of an individual. The first stage of the disorder is the prodromal stage.

This is the early stage of schizophrenia. At this stage it is not possible to diagnose schizophrenia since the symptoms are not specific. The next stage is the acute stage where the patient starts developing specific schizophrenia symptoms.

This is the active stage of the disorder and the patient after some time the patient advances to the residual stage of schizophrenia has which similar symptoms with prodromal stage.

Although the disorder is chronic it does not mean that individuals suffering from schizophrenia cannot help recover from their illnesses.

Research shows that with adequate support from the family members and community members, individuals suffering from schizophrenia can do things by their own and live responsible lives.

All that they need is adequate counseling and medication. The condition is easily treatable if it is realized in the early stages when little damage has occurred in the brain.

Therefore parents should be very observant in order to determine when their children are developing schizophrenia so that they can give them the necessary therapy, medication and support.

In order to check whether a person is developing schizophrenia, it is important to monitor whether the person like staying alone, he/she is motionless, irrational reasoning, speaks in a strange manner, over sleeping or lack of sleep and poor hygiene.

When an individual develops the above symptoms, he/she is likely to develop schizophrenia. It is therefore important to visit a psychiatrist in order to seek further clarification and take the necessary medical measures.

Types Of Schizophrenia

The ICD-10 criteria are used in the European countries but DSM-IV-TR criteria are used in the United States and rest of the world for the classification of schizophrenia. The ICD-10 criteria accentuate more on Schneiderian first-rank symptoms.

The revised fourth edition of Diagnostic and Statistical Manual of Mental Disorders (DSM-IV-TR) defines three major criteria while classifying individuals suffering from schizophrenia. Individuals suffering from this disease generally suffer from delusions, hallucinations, disorganized speech, grossly disorganized behavior and negative symptoms.

The personal relations as well as the personal life of the victim also get distracted. These signs of disturbance generally persist for about six months. Children belonging to the age group of 6 years sometimes show symptoms of this disease and they are at the risk of developing these symptoms more intensely in their adulthood. There are five types of schizophrenia each can be distinguished on the basis of the symptoms. These are:

Paranoid Schizophrenia

What Is Paranoid Schizophrenia?

Paranoid schizophrenia is a mental health condition and it's one of types of schizophrenia. Regardless of popular belief, schizophrenia doesn't cause split personalities, it in fact causes person to become split from reality, which is called psychosis.

Typical symptoms of paranoid schizophrenia are experiencing delusions or being influenced by forces that aren't real, such as other voices in your head.

Unlike other types of schizophrenia, people suffering from paranoid schizophrenia can still function in day to day life as their memory or concentration won't be massively affected.

However it affects other aspects such as dulled emotions and eccentric or weird behaviour. It is still an extremely serious condition, that if not treated can lead to major consequences such as suicidal behaviour.

Whilst paranoid schizophrenia can never be fully cured, it can be effectively treated and reduced to only infrequent episodes where the suffer will have cases of paranoid schizophrenia few and far between.

With the condition, a delusion that many sufferers experience is the feeling they're being targeted by someone or something, they often believe they're being singled out for harm.

This can mean delusions such as believing you're wanted by the authorities or even a fellow employee is trying to kill you. This is where the paranoid aspect of the condition derives from.

Another delusion many sufferers have, is the delusion of grandeur which is simple terms means a person may think they're extremely famous or friends with someone famous.

The person will carrying on believing the delusions of grandeur even when faced with powerful contrary evidence. When these delusions are challenged, the person may even become aggressive or violent.

A common misconception associated with the condition is that the sufferer has split personalities, this possibly derives from that fact the suffers often have auditory hallucinations, such as other voices in their heads.

The voices may talk to the person or possibly even talk to each other, this is an extreme symptom of the psychosis. The voices are typically unpleasant and negative, they will often make cruel or cutting comments to the sufferer. The voices also will command you to do harmful or dangerous things to other people.

If you even have one or two symptoms of the condition then it is vital that you seek immediate medial help. Paranoid schizophrenia will only get worse if left untreated, the further someone slips into psychosis the more of the person you lose.

Often sufferers will not seek medical help as everything seems so real, they don't personally feel detached from reality.

Disorganized Schizophrenia

Disorganized schizophrenia primarily involves disordered thinking. A schizophrenic patient may speak in a bunch of disorganized words. This is due to his rambled thoughts and his disorganized thinking processes.

This type of schizophrenia makes the person find his everyday tasks such as showering, brushing their teeth, and dressing themselves as difficult actions that require them more strength and care than they are able to show.

Emotional impairment often occurs; it is when they respond in a very strange way to public or private exhibitions of emotions. This type is believed to be an extreme expression of disorganization syndrome that has been assumed to be one feature a three-factor model of schizophrenic symptoms.

The other factors are reality distortion which involves delusions and hallucinations and psychomotor poverty which involves poor speech, lack of natural movement, and blunting emotions. It is often characterized by incoherent and illogical thoughts and purposeless behaviors.

Experts in schizophrenic symptoms identify this as a more severe type because the patient cannot perform day to day activities, such as taking care of his personal hygiene, preparing his meals, and other simple chores.

Patients may not be able to express the thoughts clearly because the people around them may not understand what they are saying. There is a tendency for them to become frustrated and agitated, causing them to lash out.

There are three common signs and symptoms of disorganized schizophrenia. It involves disorganized thinking, grossly disorganized behavior, and inappropriate emotional expression.

Disorganized thinking happens when a patient is having difficulty forming coherent or logical thoughts. This lack of ability greatly affects speech. For instance, a schizophrenic cannot stick to the subject, and jumps from one unrelated subject to another.

Speech disorder may become worse that it is perceived as a muddle of sounds to those who hear him. The ability to write is also severely affected by this kind of symptom.

Next is the grossly disorganized behavior that may be so severe and make the patient incapable of performing activities which include bathing, dressing properly and preparing his meals.

Strange actions such as putting on several layers of clothing during a very warm weather, displaying childlike behavior, and being or aggressive are examples of this sign.

There is an abnormal condition which is characterized by state of unconsciousness, obsession, and either rigidity or extreme flexibility of the limbs.

Also, unprovoked agitation or sexual behavior in public may occur. This behavior may feel normal to the person suffering from schizophrenia, but it appears strange to the people around them.

The last behavior focuses on lack of emotional expression of known as the flat or blunted effect. It is when a person shows the signs of normal emotions and talks with a monotonous voice. But his face appears and remains blank.

His facial expressions are very odd and drastically diminished. Sufferers of this mental disorder appear extremely apathetic. They do not have eye contact with others or any display of body language.

At times, they show inappropriate behaviors for various situations which include bursting out laughing during a sad event and crying for no apparent reason.

Catatonic Schizophrenia

Catatonic schizophrenia is also known as psychosis, a chronic mental illness which involves extreme abnormal behavior, such as being extremely hyperactive. Recognizing the signs of this condition is very important in order to get proper medication so that more serious complications can be prevented.

This mental disorder marked by symptoms such as rigidity, state of unconsciousness, excitement or mania.

Symptoms involving excitement or unconsciousness are most frequent types of behaviors typically displayed by the people suffering from schizophrenia.

A person with catatonic excitement usually experience extreme enthusiasm and display manic behaviors such as babbling or speaking without making sense, while those who experience catatonic stupor stay in a state of unconsciousness for extended periods of time.

Since this type of schizophrenia is characterized by motor symptoms, it is sometimes believed as a psychotic mood disorder.

Like the other types of mental disorder, the exact causes of catatonic schizophrenia remain unknown. But researchers noted that there is an evidence of a brain dysfunction that causes this condition.

It also involves other factors such as a person's environment, genes or brain structure may play a major part in the progression of this psychological disorder.

Researches show that the certain factors such as intake during childhood, childhood trauma, exposure to viruses as a fetus, genetics and fetus malnutrition are believed to trigger the schizophrenic symptoms.

The illness can cause a person to perceive reality in strange ways and behave inappropriately.

He may experience catatonic episode which are recognized as a severe of this disease and may last for only minutes or for many weeks.

Fortunately, this type of schizophrenia is very rare nowadays in individualized countries due to improved medications that allow faster recovery to patients.

Physical immobility is the most common symptom of the illness. It happens when a person may be unenthusiastic to move and may pose in an inflexible and rigid manner. He may choose to completely withdrawn and become unaware of his surroundings.

Another related symptom is called the waxy flexibility. It is when a person's arms or legs remain in the certain positions they are placed for long periods of time.

Experts believe that there is a loss of will and where a person responds to external stimulation and exhibit a complete lack of ability to resist. In contrast, some patients may fail their arms or move at a hyperactive pace.

When walking, they can be clumsy and may have unusual postures along with repeat certain movements.
 In some cases, patients may abandon the everyday actions, such as cleaning, cooking

and other related chores. It is necessary that family members or loved ones who are close to patients understand that this loss of drive is due to their illness, and has nothing to do with being lazy.

Moreover, hallucinations and delusions seem very realistic for the schizophrenics because many of them may continue to believe that they are not ill.

The mental disorder also affects the ability of patients to make decisions, concentrate and remember simple things. Communicating with others becomes more difficult for them.

Undifferentiated Schizophrenia

This is a catch-all category for those with schizophrenic symptoms that don't neatly fall into one of the above categories. Due to the changing nature of schizophrenia, it's quite common that someone will be diagnosed this way at some point.

Residual Schizophrenia

Among the subtypes of schizophrenia, residual schizophrenia is considered as the negative type of this mental disorder. People suffering from the illness usually lose their interest in their lives and do not interact with the other folks and show irritation.

A person with this disorder is affected by the other major types of schizophrenia such as the paranoid, undifferentiated, and catatonic schizophrenia.

The symptoms can be found out from the fact whether the person is displaying the other characteristics such as delusions, hallucinations or other mental disorder.

In addition, the residual schizophrenia is not identified as a dangerous type as it is usually discovered during the last stage of the diagnosis.
Generally, the disorder is diagnosed when the patient no longer exhibits prominent schizophrenic symptoms. In such cases, symptoms have reduced in severity.

Although hallucinations, delusions or idiosyncratic behaviors may still occur, the manifestations are significantly lessened in comparison to the acute stage of the illness.

Schizophrenic symptoms and their ramifications are diverse. They can give different kinds of impairment which affect the patient's life to various degrees. Patients require custodial care in state institutions, while other sufferers are still employed and maintain an active family life.

On the other hand, most patients are at neither of these extremes. Most of them will have a waxing and waning course marked with some health care organizations and some assistance from external support sources.

People with a higher level of functioning prior to the beginning of their illness usually have a better outcome. Generally, these outcomes are associated with short episodes of symptoms worsening followed by a normal performance.

However, researches show that women have a better prognosis for higher functioning than men.

On the contrary, a poorer prognosis is showed by a gradual or subtle onset, which starts during childhood or adolescence; abnormalities in brain structure, as seen on imaging studies; and failure to return to prior levels of performance after severe episodes.

This type of schizophrenia is typically diagnosed by various symptoms. First are the prominent "negative" symptoms which involve reduction of physical movements in an individual, blunting of affect, passivity, poverty of quantity or content of speech, poor nonverbal communication by facial expression, lack of eye contact, and poor posture, poor self-care and social performance.
Second is the evidence in the past of at least one psychotic episode such as radical changes in personality and impaired functioning meeting the diagnostic criteria of the mental illness.

Next symptom occurs during a period of at least one year in which the intensity and frequency of symptoms like delusions and hallucinations have been significantly reduced and the "negative" schizophrenic syndrome has been there.

The last is the lack of dementia or other organic brain disorder, as well as of constant depression or institutionalism enough to explain the negative impairments.

History

The term schizophrenia is in practice since 1911. It was finally kept in the category of mental illness in 1887 by Emil Kraepelin.

The Ancient Egyptian, Hindu, Chinese, Greek, and Roman writings also describe about this disorder. During the medieval times schizophrenia was thought to be caused by spirits and evil powers.
Studies have specified that the social stigma is one of the treacherous obstacles that stop the patients of schizophrenia from recovering.

A study carried out in 1999 designated that about 12.8% Americans who were suffering from schizophrenia were more interested violent activities while 48% individuals were calm and quite.

A very famous Hollywood film entitled The Beautiful Mind depicts the life of John Nash who suffers from paranoid schizophrenia. Another film The Soloist portrays about the challenges faced by Juilliard-trained musician Nathaniel Ayers as a result of schizophrenia.

History of Schizophrenia - Origination and Meaning

Schizophrenia is a type of mental disorder in which a person suffers from distorted perception of real life and very often losing touch with reality. Originating from the Geek word: schizo (split) and phrene (mind), it is a mental disorder with a long history.

Schizophrenia in 2000B.C.

The history of Schizophrenia dated back to around 2000 B.C., when little was known about mental disorders. It was believed that the person who is suffering from mental disturbances has been invaded by an evil spirit and the only way to cure the disorder is by driving out the evil spirit. In those times, there were many types of exorcism method.

One was to made patients listen to music in order to drive the evil spirit out, another brutal one see patients skull being drill to provide a way for the spirits to get out.

Schizophrenia as understood by the Egyptians

A mention of mental disorders and their symptoms is there in The Book of Heart, an Egyptian book. The Egyptians believed that the heart and brain are interlinked.

Therefore, according to their belief, a person who is suffering from certain mental disorder must be suffering from certain heart problems as well.

All the people suffering from Schizophrenia were considered mad and dangerous, in spite of the display of their normal human characteristics at all other times.

The only refuges for them were the mental homes. Such misunderstanding stayed for a very long time before researchers came up with a scientific explanation to dispel the misconception.

Evolution in the understanding of Schizophrenia

Initial efforts to understand and record atypical mental behaviors were made in the seventeenth century.

Later in 1887, Emile Kraepelin, a German psychiatrist, started to record and put into place the different types of mental disorders and defined them by one term: dementia praecox. It was not until the nineteenth century before people begin to gain more awareness about diseases and their causes.

It was not until the turn of the century before we saw many new medical science breakthrough findings. Schizophrenia, as a mental illness was coined by a Swiss psychiatrist named Eugen Bleuler in 1908.

The definition and symptoms of Schizophrenia that we are using today was put up by another German psychiatrist,Kurt Schneider, in 1957.

Regardless of the progression in medical science, there were few people who were unable to accept the logic and explanation of science and for their benefit continued to commit cruelty towards human race, one such example is the case of World War II.

During the World War II Schizophrenia was identified to be a genetic disorder and in order to prevent transmission of the condition from one generation to another and practice selective procreation, mentally disturbed people were killed.

Despite of such pathetic examples in the history of Schizophrenia, psychiatrists, doctors and scientists have never given up hope and have worked day and night for advancement in the understanding of Schizophrenia. Many misconceptions about Schizophrenia have become clear.

Today, instead of brutally treating the patients, considering the patients mad and sending them to asylum, society is becoming able to accept the fact that such patients need understanding and sympathy. To help treat and relieve their mental disorder, you need to spend time, show care and affection with proper medication.

Causes of Schizophrenia

The brain has one of the most complex structure and operation in the world. It is no surprise that mankind has been trying to figure out how it function for the longest time and could manage to find out only very little.

This is the case of Schizophrenia as well, a mental disorder that affects one's perception of the real world. Researchers have been studying the condition for a considerably time and could only come out with relatively little findings on the causes of this mental disorder listed below.

Genetic and Environmental aspects

Genetic factors play an important role in the occurrence of Schizophrenia. Studies have proven that a person with family history of Schizophrenia is more likely to develop the mental disorder himself.

Statistics in terms of propensity to develop Schizophrenia show that people with family history of Schizophrenia is rated 10% where as people without family history of Schizophrenia is rated at 1%.

Both genetic as well as environmental factors play a strategic role in the development of schizophrenia. People with family history of the disease are at the risk of getting distressed with the disease in near future.

However, the guesstimates of heritability vary due to difficulty in separating the genetic as well as environmental factors while identifying the disease.

According to an estimate about 40% of the mono-zygotic twins are at the risk of getting infected with this disease. Many genes are associated with development of every symptom of the disorder.

A number of genome wide associations like zinc finger protein 804A, NOTCH4 and protein loci are found to be linked. There appears a momentous overlap between the genetics of schizophrenia and bipolar disorder.

The environmental factors that are linked with schizophrenia include living environment, prenatal stressors and drug intake. Social isolation and immigration related to social adversity, racial discrimination, family dysfunction, unemployment, and poor housing conditions also play a crucial role in the development of this disorder.

Childhood factors like sexual abuse and any trauma can result in schizophrenia in the adulthood.

However genetic factor is just an influencing factor and not a determining factor. Supporting this, 60% of people who suffer from Schizophrenia were found to have no family history of the disorder.

Looking into the environmental aspect of the causes responsible for Schizophrenia, scientists have indicated that an elevated level of stress is accountable for triggering Schizophrenia, as increased stress not only causes several biochemical changes in the body but also increases the level of cortisol hormone.

Complications And Insufficient Care During Pregnancy And Delivery

Children born after complications in delivery are more likely to have Schizophrenia. If there are complications during delivery, this can lead to hypoxia in the neonatal brain resulting in higher possibility of the child getting Schizophrenia when he grows up. This finding was supported by animal model, epidemiological, molecular and genetic studies. Proper care during pregnancy to avoid stress and keep a good diet is an important factor.

Studies have shown that mothers who starve or are having malnutrition are likely to give birth to a child suffering from Schizophrenia.
Through a study on pregnant ladies during Winter War of 1939, in Finland, it was elucidated that those pregnant women who knew about their husband's death during pregnancy and hence underwent a lot of stress were more susceptible to give birth to a child with Schizophrenia, than the women who knew about their husband's death after delivery.

During pregnancy, mothers who develop viral infections such as maternal genital infection are more likely to have a child who has a higher change to get Schizophrenia.

Neurological aspects

Several structural and functional changes in the brain can cause Schizophrenia. The frontal lobe, part of the brain that helps human to make decision is malfunction. Researches have long proved that people with Schizophrenia have usually large ventricles, indicating a discrepancy in their neurons.

A number of drugs namely cocaine, cannabis and amphetamines also contribute in the development of schizophrenia. Individuals suffering from schizophrenia normally consume drugs in order to cope up with depression, loneliness, boredom and anxiety. Cannabis is generally associated with increasing the risk of development of a psychotic disorder.

Frequent use of this drug generally doubles the risk of getting affected with schizophrenia and psychosis. Excessive intake of cocaine and amphetamine can also increase the risk of schizophrenia.

Other factors like hypoxia and infection, stress or malnutrition in the mother during fetal development can somewhat increase the risk of schizophrenia in the baby in later stages of life.

Studies have indicated that the people suffering from schizophrenia are generally born in the months of winter and spring and are at the risk of getting infected with viral diseases more frequently. The percentage of such individuals varies from 5-8%.

Chapter II

What are the symptoms of Schizophrenia?

Schizophrenia symptoms start showing up between the ages of 16 to 30. In some of the cases, children have Schizophrenia too. Schizophrenia symptoms are of three types namely positive symptoms, negative symptoms, and cognitive symptoms.

Positive Symptoms

Positive Schizophrenia Symptoms are symptoms that are psychotic in nature and are not usually seen in a healthy person. All positive symptoms involve losing touch with reality. Some of the positive symptoms seen in patients with Schizophrenia include

Hallucinations

Hallucinations are usually sounds or some other perceptions encountered as true once they exist only inside the individual's thoughts. Although hallucinations may include any of the 5 sensory faculties, auditory hallucinations like hearing voices or several other noises are most typical in this condition.

Visual hallucinations are likewise common. Study shows that auditory hallucinations take place whenever individuals misunderstand their personal intrinsic self-talk as provided by an external source. Hallucinations also have a tendency to get more serious when the patient is all alone.

Delusions

Delusions are false ideas that seem real to the patient even though strong evidence exists that they don't. Some patients think they are famous social figures, some think that someone is trying to spy on them.

Disorganized Behavior

Schizophrenic patients experience behaviors like unprovoked and inappropriate outbursts, uninhibited and impulsive actions.

Patients have problems with hygiene or selecting appropriate clothes as per the weather. Patients may feel agitated, tense, and anxious without any apparent reason.

- A drop in total everyday performance
- Unstable or unsuitable psychological reactions
- Actions which seem weird and have no reason
- Absence of self-consciousness as well as impulse control

Disordered Thinking and Speech

Losing thought during conversations, giving answers that are not related to the questions, jumping from one topic to another without apparent logical reasons are some of the actions that portray Disordered Thinking in affected patients.

Disordered Speech includes actions like Individuals creating their own sounds and words that do not actually exist and doesn't make sense. They may keep repeating words and ideas without a reason and may speak a lot without getting to the point and providing irrelevant and unnecessary details.

• Negative Symptoms

Negative Schizophrenia Symptoms are related to disturbances to normal behaviors and emotions. Some of the common and strong negative symptoms portrayed by patients suffering from Schizophrenia include

• Affective Flattening:

This is a very common symptom seen in schizophrenic patients. Patients with this symptom portray relatively unresponsive and immobile facial expressions. This is usually accompanied by poor eye contact and reduced body movement and body language.

• Alogia:

Alogia is trouble with speaking due to mental defect. Patients affected with Schizophrenia demonstrate a reduction in verbal fluency and total speech output. Sometimes the patients struggle even with giving brief answers to questions.

• Avolition:

Avolition refers to a lack of desire or will to take part in activities. This also involves loss of motivation. Patients demonstrate avolition in different ways. Some patients portray indifference towards their surroundings and sit still for long periods of time. Some patients display a lack of interest in social activities or work.

• Cognitive Symptoms

Cognitive Schizophrenia Symptoms are subtle for some and severe for others. Some of the cognitive symptoms commonly seen include

• *Dementia:*

Schizophrenia in patients causes Dementia. Dementia affects that part of the brain that is used for memory, language, learning, decision making, thinking, and reasoning.

• Reduced Executive Functioning:

People affected by Schizophrenia experience reduced executive functioning. This means they have trouble in paying adequate attention, manage time, plan and organize, switch focus and remember details. Affected patients have problems in maintaining relationships and doing things independently. Day to day functioning becomes difficult for affected people.

• Attention Deficit:

Schizophrenic patients experience difficulty in focusing and paying attention.

Schizophrenia cannot be cured but a careful diagnosis and lifelong treatment can help the impacted patients to enhance the quality of their life. Constant care and support are extremely integral to help a Schizophrenic patient survive and live a better life.

Differences Between Positive and Negative Schizophrenia Symptoms

Positive and negative symptoms are a common characteristic of a Schizophrenia patient.

Positive Symptoms

Positive symptoms define all symptoms which are more specific to Schizophrenic patients and are not normally experienced by healthy individuals. These symptoms pertain to loss of touch with the real life. Positive symptoms can be either severe or mild which are unnoticeable by people around. Positive systems include delusions, illusions, hallucinations and having nebulous thinking.

Negative Symptoms

Negative symptoms define all symptoms that can occur in any healthy individual in response to certain emotional or physical setback. Negative symptoms are not blatantly noticeable and are hard to identify. Different instances of negative symptoms are:

Dullness in the mood and voice of a person:

The person may not display any expressions on his face and speak in a monotonous tone.

Depression and loss of pleasure in day to day life:

The person loses interest in any activity, feels hopeless, helpless, miserable and pathetic, experiences guilt, and has constant self depreciation thoughts in his mind. Such a person does not feel enthusiastic or interested in anything in spite of rewards, recognitions or encouragement.

Lack of concentration in the activities of day to day life:

The person is not motivated, undergoes loss of enthusiasm and loses concentration in many activities.

Emotional imbalance and social withdrawal:

The person experiences lack of emotion and loses connection with his loved ones. The person is unable to respond to any external emotional stimuli. Such a person is susceptible to cry at a wedding or laugh while attending a funeral. He likes to spend time alone and will choose not to talk to anyone even when he is encouraged to do so.

Failure to articulate:

As the frontal lobe of the brain is affected in Schizophrenia, the person's ability to articulate and understand things or complex issues is severely hampered.

Incompetence in planning, organizing and following instructions:

The person is unable to perform planning or organize things in an orderly manner. He will find it challenging to organize and express his thoughts when communicating to people.

Henc, it becomes very difficult for a normal individual to understand a Schizophrenic patient who sounds very confusing, illogical and unclear in certain situations. Schizophrenia patients can find it challenging to follow basic instructions and perform simple jobs.

Loss of appetite:

The person has loss of appetite and does not feel like eating even if he has not had any food for long and his body requires it.

Lack of personal hygiene

The person becomes very lazy and seems like he cannot take care of himself. He will even neglect his personal grooming like bathing and cleaning himself.

Violent behaviors

Generally, this symptom is observed only in Schizophrenic patients who have been short tempered or who have committed crimes in the past. In cases of Schizophrenia patients, these violent behaviors worsen.

Talking about self destruction

The person might talk about committing suicide. When such incident happens, the patient must be taken seriously and medical attention is needed immediately.

Mechanisms associated with schizophrenia

Dopamine

Dopamine is a type of neurotransmitter, found in humans and animals and is responsible for the activation of different dopamine receptors. There is a prominent level of dopamine in the brain of a person suffering from Schizophrenia. In the past, post mortem analysis of Schizophrenic patients has shown an increase in the dopamine receptor - D2 in the inner region of the forebrain known as the striatum. These increased levels of D2 receptor increase the intensity of signals in the brain and is responsible for the symptoms of hallucination, illusion, paranoia and obsession.

Neurotrophins

Neurotrophins are proteins which help in the repair, continued existence and development of neurons. They are actually growth factors which are released by a stimulated, active neuron and help neurons in establishing connections with surrounding neurons. As we age, our brain executes a maintenance mechanism according to which neurons are not useful i.e. the ones which do not have connection with surrounding neurons are eliminated through the process of programmed cell death.

The secretion of neurotrophins is essential for the prevention of the cell apoptosis or programmed cell death of its target neuron.

In a Schizophrenic patient, neurotrophins are in much reduced amount as a result when the maintenance mechanism of the brain is executed most of the neurons undergo programmed cell death and there is neuronal degeneration.

Studies have also demonstrated that a reduction in the computational capability is associated with reduced neutrophin level in the brain. Experimental results have shown a reduction of 5% in the gray matter volume in the cortex region of the brain of Schizophrenic patients.

Glutamate

Glutamate also known as Glutamic acid is a common neurotransmitter found in the brain.

A postmortem study of Schizophrenic patient has shown a reduction in the density of glutamate receptor in the brain of the patient.

Such an activity of glutamate holds up to the finding of increased levels of dopamine receptors in Schizophrenic patients, because dopamine receptors have an inherent property of restraining glutamate.

Hypoxia

Hypoxia is a term used to define a lack of oxygen supply either to one part of the body or to all the parts. The human brain stands apart for its major consumption of oxygen.

Studies have elucidated the reason behind the sensitivity of the brain for its level of oxygen. Studies have shown that even though the weight of brain is only 2% of the entire body weight but the amount of oxygen the brain consumes is as much as 20% of the oxygen consumed by the entire human body.

Hypoxia in the brain also known as cerebral ischemia and can be either due to accidental head injury or due to depreciated activity of nerve cells as a result of excessive addictive drug consumption.

Under hypoxia there is an entry of excessive amounts of calcium, which is responsible for intracellular excitation waves, into the neurons, these cause severe harms to the neurons and the connections of the neurons and in some cases can result in the death of the neuron.

Schizophrenic patients who are under great stress due to sarcasm, hallucinations, delusions, nebulous thinking, mood swings and experience traumas in their lives are more likely to experience cerebral ischemia and as a result of which there can be an increased level of intracellular excitation.

An elevated intracellular excitation leads to destruction of the complex neural circuitry and this hampers the cognitive functions of the brain.

Diagnosis

At present there is no definite test available that can assure that a particular person is suffering from schizophrenia. The health practitioners gather information from the medical, family and medical-health backgrounds in order to diagnose this disorder.

The practitioner can also perform some sort of physical tests in order to check the symptoms of this disorder.

The medical examination includes some lab tests in order to get an idea of the patient's health. Mental health professionals deal with the symptoms like hallucinations, delusions, depression, anxiety or physical abuse. Some symptoms of schizophrenia can also occur in other disorders like the bipolar disorder, anxiety disorder and personality disorder.

Any disorder associated with abnormal behavior, mood or thinking for example borderline personality disorder or dissociative identity disorder (DID) commonly known as multiple personality disorder (MPD) are generally difficult to be distinguished from schizophrenia.

The mental-health professionals can also perform mental test examinations. Patients of schizophrenia are at elevated risk of getting affected with anxiety or depression disorder and of committing suicide.

Medications

A number of treatments are yet available but medication plays a key role in treating schizophrenia. These medications are known as anti-psychotics as they reduce the intensity of the psychotic symptoms.

Many health care professionals prescribe a combined dose of these medications along with the psychiatric drugs in order to provide benefit to the patient.

Medications that are beneficial in dealing with the positive symptoms of this disorder are olanzapine, risperidone, quetiapine, paliperidone and asinapine. These drugs are also known as second generation anti-psychotics. These drugs act faster in comparison to the psychiatric medications.

These anti-psychotic drugs also suffer from some side effects including dizziness, sleepiness and increased appetite. Weight gain, high blood sugar levels, increased blood lipid levels and sometimes higher level of prolactin hormone have been noticed. The medications that are useful in treating the symptoms of schizophrenia may not be equally effective in treating the symptoms of the disorder in childhood.

Mood stabilizer medications like lithium, carbamazepine and lamotrigine can be used to deal with mood fluctuations in addition to psychotic symptoms. These medications take a longer time to show their effect in addition to the anti-psychotic drugs.

These drugs can cause birth defects if taken by pregnant women. Antidepressant medications can be taken in order to deal with depression in schizophrenia.

The common antidepressants are serotonergic medications that affect the serotonin levels and the common examples are fluoxetine, paroxetine, citalopram and duloxetine. Electroconvulsive therapy (ECT) is a better option for the patients who show inadequate result while treating with medication trials as well as psychosocial interventions.

While dealing with pregnant women with schizophrenia the health professions become more cautious and take extra care of the patient. Some medications can increase the risk of damage to fetus and during breast feeding so the health professionals try to overcome these factors.

Educating the family members about the symptoms, course and treatment of schizophrenia comes under the category of psycho-education. This tool includes family support, problem solving skills and help from care-providers at the time of crisis.

This intervention has given better results if continued for several months as it decreases the problems associated with emotional and social stresses. The burden over the family members is also reduced as with the help of health experts the family relationship of the patient also improves.

Assertive community treatment (ACT) is another intervention which consists of meeting of the health experts with the patient in community settings rather than home or home.

The team of health professionals is made up of a variety of experts for example, a psychiatrist, nurse, case manager, employment counselor and substance abused counselor. This tool is helpful in the treatment of patients who are either hospitalized or become homeless.

Medical and psychosocial interventions focusing on substance abuse are integral part of treatment that specifically deals with the patients of schizophrenia. According to an estimate about 50% patients of schizophrenia suffer from some kind of substance abuse or dependence.

Social skill training is another important tool that teaches e important skills to the patients so that they can handle social situations easily. This treatment is helpful for the patients that resist using drugs.

Supported employment provides support like a work coach, interviewing for jobs and education and support for the employers to hire individuals with chronic medical illness.

This treatment helps the patients to work for prolong hours. Cognitive behavioral therapy is a reality based intervention that helps a client to deal with all the problems that interfere with his or her ability to interact with others.

This tool helps to improve social relationships of the individual. This intervention can be performed individually or in group sessions. By educating the patients about the side effects of the anti-psychotic drugs the body weight of the patient can be managed.

Prognosis

According to a report presented in 2011 about 24 million people are suffering from schizophrenia. This disorder occurs 1.4 times more frequently in males as compared to that in females. The peak ages for the onset of symptoms of the disorder are 20-28 years for males and 26-32 for females.

The onset of the symptoms of the disorder is generally rare in childhood but may arise in later stages. The percentage of occurrence of schizophrenia varies in different nations. The patients are at a double risk of death than the normal individuals. Almost half of the patients suffer from substance abuse during their lifetime.

Current status

Cognitive remediation is in use now-a-days as it helps the individuals with schizophrenia to deal with the cognitive problems. Vocational rehabilitation deals with increasing the efficiency of the patient to deal with social situations.

Peer-to-peer treatment is a promising intervention as it helps the individuals of schizophrenia to develop constructive involvement. More research is required to deal with the weight management problems.

Chapter III

Living and Coping With Schizophrenia

Schizophrenia is a mental disorder which has no permanent cure. Its symptoms can be dormant in one moment while severely aggravated in other moments, depending on the effectiveness of the medications and treatments the Schizophrenic patient is taking.

Schizophrenia is very detrimental as it takes away loved ones, family, friends and sometimes one's ability to make a living. In order to live life again, it is important for Schizophrenic patients to learn how to cope this dreadful disorder. Following are some of the suggestions which can be used for coping and living with Schizophrenia.

Acceptance of the Reality

The patient must admit the fact that he is suffering from Schizophrenia. Usually, a

Schizophrenic patient denies his suffering. He thinks that people are lying to him; this is because of basic human tendency of refusal to things which prove one wrong.

As the same time, Schizophrenia patient suffer from hallucinations which make it extremely challenging for him to differentiate between real life and illusion.

To handle this situation, families must lend their supporting hand to manage his medication taking and making sure he attends his psychotherapy session.

The patient should also be sent for group therapy where he is made to realize that if he admits that he is suffering from the mental illness, it will make his life and others around him far easier. The patient who has admitted to reality is more likely to take his medications on time, discuss openly during psychotherapy sessions and gain the most out of all his treatments.

Knowledge about Schizophrenia

Knowledge about Schizophrenia is no doubt very important in order to cope with it. Patient with Schizophrenia will be in a better position to cope with the illness if they fully understand it.

Family members will also be more understanding of the situation and response better to the patient. Hence, it is vastly important for the patient and family members to learn about the symptoms associated with Schizophrenia.

Living independently in a safe neighborhood

A Schizophrenic patient whose family members refuse to take care of him either due to lack of understanding or lack of funds can possibly live in an independent setting depending on the severity of his condition. However, it is vital for him to take his medication and visit his psychotherapist on time.

Whenever possible, neighbors can also help to show some care and concern to make sure he takes his medications.

Living with Family or in a Hospital

It is advisable for a Schizophrenic patient to live with his family or in a hospital whenever possible. This is so that family members or medical professionals can keep track of the patient and make sure that he is taking his medications, attending group therapy sessions and meetings his psychotherapist on time.

They can also keep track of the patient's behavior and see if it has improve over time.

A Schizophrenia patient who gets enough love, care and support from families are less likely to suffer from paranoid attack; it definitely makes it easier for him to live and cope with Schizophrenia.

Schizophrenia Treatment, Is It Should Be Done With Much Patience

Schizophrenia is a serious mental illness, which has many reasons for its occurrence. There are many stages of this illness, and treatment should be given after a efficient study is done on the case.

Schizophrenia treatment should not be considered frivolously. Only a professional, skilled doctor be supposed to engage in treating a schizophrenia patient.

Very often schizophrenia patients are stubborn and uncontrollable. nevertheless with proper, timely medication this sickness possibly will be controlled.

Schizophrenia treatment involves many medications. but psychosocial interventions too is needed when schizophrenia is been treated for. The needed type of treatment differs from person to person.

Schizophrenia is not a permanently curable sickness. Schizophrenia treatment is done with the meaning of managing the symptoms and improving the condition. Permanent cure of schizophrenia is not recorded as yet and according to medical experts it cannot be depended upon

Laboratory tests are not available to diagnose schizophrenia. Yet, brain abnormalities associated with schizophrenia could be detected by doing brain imaging studies akin to MRI or CT scans.

There are many supportive treatments for schizophrenia. An antipsychotic is a schizophrenia treatment and the basis for the work antipsychotic is they help decrease the intensity of psychotic symptom s.

The term second generation antipsychotic is used to refer to the newer faction of medication for schizophrenia and drugs like quetiapine, olanzapine, risperidone and ziprasidone belong to this class.

Among many other psychiatric medications, these newer medications are known for having the ability of working more quickly.

The unhealthy side effects of schizophrenia treatment medication could be dizziness, sleepiness, and increased appetite. Weight add too is a problematic side effect which could result in high blood sugar levels, raised blood lipid levels, and even increased levels of a hormone called prolactin.

Given that there are many potential side effects like muscle stiffness, shakiness and very rarely uncoordinated muscle twitches that can be lasting, doctors closely monitor their patients after treatment.

The above mentioned side effects may mostly take place with the use of the older type of antipsychotic medications such as haloperidol, perphenazine, and molindine.

All schizophrenia treatment medications which are used on adult patients are not accepted in using for childhood schizophrenia.

Individuals with a diagnosable mood turmoil in addition to psychotic symptoms such as schizoaffective and depression too are now and again treated with mood stabilizer medications like lithium, divalproex, carbamazepine and lamotrigne etc. which are mostly supposed to be schizophrenia treatment medications.

Chapter IV

Dealing With Schizophrenia as a Caregiver

A caregiver usually serves as the nucleus of support for anyone suffering from schizophrenia, particularly while going through the most trying times caused due to symptoms of this disease.

Thus, it is very important for the caregiver to provide motivation and encouragement to the patient, as well as act as a benchmark of reality for the patient, providing them with a calmer and more pleasant view of the world around them.

It is also important for a Caregiver of a person with a mental illness to realize that their patient requires regular monitoring and supervision of qualified healthcare professionals and that one cannot take care of the schizophrenia patient alone.

A Caregiver of a mentally ill patient has many responsibilities. At times they are just

so overwhelming and seemingly out of
control, but at other times when the patient
is not so unwell it is just a matter of
overseeing routine and appointments rather
than having to be hands-on involved.

Understanding Schizophrenia in Children and Adolescents

For aptly understanding of childhood and
adolescent Schizophrenia, parents must
consult psychiatrist who has experience in
dealing with children and adolescents. There
are few instances when one might get
confused whether a child has Schizophrenia
or not:

- **Having imaginary friends and talking to unreal things**

  It is common for children to have
  imaginary friends that they play or talk
  with when they are around three years
  old; this is a fairly normal
  characteristic of children at this age.
  However, if such a characteristic is

found in a 12 years old child or in a 15 years old adolescent, then parents need to be concerned, they must talk to the child and understand what he is feeling and must consult a pediatrician or a psychologist.

• **Grievance of losing a friend or family**

An adolescent can feel sad over losing family member or a close friend, among other things. He might try to avoid going out and talk to anyone. At this time, it is common for people around the child to be unsure if he is suffering from Schizophrenia, especially if the family has history of the mental disorder. At this point of time, it is recommended to talk to the adolescent and bring him in to a psychiatrist for counseling. The symptoms displayed can be either due to temporary depression or early onset of Schizophrenia.

Symptoms of Schizophrenia in Children and Adolescents

In accordance to the psychosocial development studies done by Erik Erikson, humans below the age of 13 are classified as children and those between the ages of 13 and 19 are classified as adolescents. Childhood or adolescent Schizophrenia crops up in the early years of life; it is rare but is more troublesome to manage.

A child or adolescent suffering from Schizophrenia cannot function normally like others. His ability to think, take decisions and understand things is severely hampered. A child suffering from Schizophrenia can be as young as 8 years.

Children and adolescents with Schizophrenia suffer from hallucinations, delusions and distorted thinking, similar symptoms to an adult Schizophrenic patient, except few small variations.
There can be a gradual shift in the behavior pattern of a child or adolescent with Schizophrenia. From having predictable

behaviors, the children can display unpredictably bad behaviors.

Children with Schizophrenia tend to stick with their parents all the time, they do not enjoy playing and chatting with other kids, they lose interest in most of the activities, face difficulty in concentrating on studies and their school performance degrades.

School teachers are often first to notice their aberrant behavior first.

Treatment

To treat children and adolescents with Schizophrenia, group therapy, family therapy and atypical antipsychotic drugs are commonly used.

The common practice is for parents to bring their child to a pediatrician and ask him to refer a psychiatrist who is good in diagnosing, assessing and treating children with Schizophrenia.

Parents must try their best to encourage the child to participate in different activities in school that help to treat the mental disorder.

Tips to Lower Risk of Schizophrenia in Children

Ignoring the symptoms of schizophrenia and leaving it untreated can lead to severe complications. It is a mental disorder that affects a person's behavior and the way he feels and thinks. A schizophrenic loses touch with reality.

Schizophrenia runs in the genes, but it is not necessary that everyone in the family of an affected person would inherit the disease. It only increases the probability of its occurrence.

Almost 85 percent people do not inherit schizophrenia despite having someone in the family suffering from it, while there are also those who get it even when there is no family history.

Reasons other than genetics

Besides genetics, there are other reasons that can trigger schizophrenia in an individual:

- Pregnancy complications, traumatic experiences in childhood such as sexual abuse, psychological abuse, and brain injury are also contributing factors that could lead to schizophrenia.

- Abusing illicit drugs at an early age also precipitates the onset of the disease.

- Any discordant and strained relationship with family members is also said to be a major reason for schizophrenia.

- Environment and life situations also hasten the development of the disorder in an individual. A poor person is more vulnerable to get the disease than a prosperous one.

Incidentally, there are also reports which predict high occurrences of schizophrenia in rich countries as well. Seeking the best of treatments like the schizophrenia treatment can be a viable option for patients. The schizophrenia disorder treatment is counted among the best in the country.

However, when there is a family history of schizophrenia, certain precautions become necessary to prevent or lessen the effects of schizophrenia for the rest, especially the children.

Because landing up in a schizophrenia treatment center cannot be a desirable situation for anybody, even if it is the reputed schizophrenia treatment.

Following are a few tips that would help in keeping the children safe from getting the disease:

Extending love and support to children:

If there is a family history of schizophrenia, children in such households should be treated with utmost love and care. Any confrontation, abuse of mental, physical and emotional should be avoided at all cost. Such harsh behavior of parents and elders could trigger symptoms of schizophrenia in them.

Forging friendly relationship with kids:

A friendly relationship with the children and helping them make friends outside can prevent them from feeling isolated. It will boost their self-esteem and thwart the advancement of schizophrenia signs. It is especially true of teenagers in the family.

Keeping kids occupied

The children should be encouraged to involve more into activities, like art and crafts, sports, music or other activities. Engagement will help them enhance their cognitive and emotional quotients.

Teaching them to manage stress

Handing out lessons to children on how to manage stress will go a long way. Coping with stress can really help keep schizophrenia at bay. These learned skills will hold them in good stead later in life.

Nurturing their physical health

Right from choosing a healthy diet rich in nutrients to encouraging adequate physical activity, and nurturing a good physical health in the children will act as a deterrence to the onset of schizophrenia. They should be shielded and protected from getting any head injuries.

Giving them foods rich in omega-3 fatty acids

Researches have found that omega-3 fatty acids, or fish oil, may decrease the risk of psychotic disorders. Children should be given enough fishes like salmon, tuna, herrings and mackerel as they are rich in omega-3 fatty acids. Vegetarians can try flax seeds which are a good source of omega-3 fatty acids.

Chapter V

How Does Schizophrenia Manifest?

When a child is diagnosed with schizophrenia parents are shocked because they can not understand how come a child that is intelligent, and looks good could be that ill.

Schizophrenia comes with symptoms just like any other disease but they differ from person to person. Some people might have just one episode of schizophrenia in their entire life, but in others schizophrenia might manifest more frequent and for a long period of time.

The first who notice there is something wrong with a person are the family members. They see that the person is not like it used to be any more and go for a check up at the doctor's.

Because schizophrenia gives perceptual difficulties the ill person might refuse contact with strangers and will isolate himself from others.

They will become less interested in their usual activities including work and personal hygiene and this will alert their family members that something is wrong.

Schizophrenia gives changes in personality at first only minor changes but after some time quite obvious changes. The inability of showing emotions like crying or laughing will install after a while and if they manage to laugh they make it in a strange way that makes it inappropriate.

They become indifferent to others and to social activities and they end up isolating themselves.

A disorder in thoughts will install in most of the cases and the ill persons will not be able to concentrate as they used to and will forget a lot of things.

They generally develop a problem with talking, they use odd language structures.

They always seem confused and jump from
a topic to another.

Some might become hyperactive and will
develop intense preoccupations with religion
believing that they have a special mission,
will write non stop meaningless phrases, and
might use drugs and alcohol. Some develop
extreme reactions to criticism and will even
try to run away from home.

Due to the perceptual changes in their brain,
the ill person might see, feel and smell
things that are not there, that are not real. All
these manifestations are hallucinations.

In the worse cases they might attempt to
suicide or to auto-mutilate because they
seem to hear voices telling them to do that.
All their senses are turned upside down and
sometimes even a telephone ring might be
confused for a fire alarm and provoke
agitation among them.

The schizophrenic people realize that they
have problems with their senses but they try
to hide all the symptoms away, they will

keep it a secret. They will deny all these facts and will avoid any situation that puts them face in face with the fact that they are different.

These ill persons are even more afraid that they will be abandoned by the loved ones and that is why family must always stand beside them and support them. All they need is love, patience and a lot of understanding.

Advice For Getting Treatment For Schizophrenia

People are not born with schizophrenic symptoms. They can appear as early as age 16 or as late as 40 with the typical age around 19. If you feel that you are losing your mind or if your family and friends are showing concern that you have these problems that were listed in the introduction, be open to getting help.

Most forms of schizophrenia respond well to medications. Find a qualified psychiatrist to prescribe medications by calling your insurance or Google. If you do not have insurance many doctors will be willing to work a payment plan.

People with schizophrenia respond well to cognitive behavioral therapy. This is a therapy that includes examining your thoughts, choosing more appropriate and helpful thoughts and beliefs, and changing your behaviors to ones that will keep you safe and functioning well.

Look online and find one in your area who treats schizophrenia. You can also call your insurance.

Your family and/or people you live with can be helpful. They can remind you to take your medications, they can guide you if you have a delusion or hallucination by gently helping you question it.
You may wish to have one or more supportive people participate in a therapy session with you so the therapist can train them how to help you.

With schizophrenia you may always need to be on medication and you may need therapy or case management throughout your life. Sometimes you might be tempted to discontinue therapy or medication if you are faring well.

Many people with schizophrenia lead happy and productive lives when they stay on their medication and get the help that they need.

Schizophrenia is an illness just like depression, anxiety, bipolar, the flu, etc. and it does not have to define who you are. You can look at what you are good at and what you are accomplishing in your life and see yourself as that and you happen to have an illness called schizophrenia.

When someone becomes aware that they have schizophrenia, they often think that they will never work, have a family, and do the things that others do.

After receiving therapy for schizophrenia, often people can move from hospitalization to employment, marriage, and parenthood. It does not have to stop you from living a full and rewarding life.

People with schizophrenia have a behavior similar to people with depression and anxiety. They isolate themselves from the world, and from the people who could help them.

Your family and friends can help you once they understand what you are going through.

Earlier in this article it mentions the ages of the onset of schizophrenia. If you are 19 years old or under 40 it is not necessary to worry about getting it.

Often, people will get anxious that they have schizophrenia because they fall within the onset ages. There is no way to predict who will get it, so why worry?
 Although you need medication and therapy, give yourself credit for being able to live a normal and successful life. It comes back to the idea that you are not schizophrenia, you are a person who has schizophrenia and you are also many other things.

Treatment for schizophrenia

The American Psychiatric Association publication 'Guidelines for the Treatment of Patients with Schizophrenia' states: "Antipsychotic medications are indicated for nearly all acute psychotic episodes in patients with schizophrenia."

There is also a significant overlap in terms of the medications for schizophrenia and bipolar disorder (Manic Depression).

There are two main classifications of medications (from a layman's perspective); the traditional antipsychotic medications (Haldol, etc.), and the newer, 'atypical' antipsychotic medications that have come out in the past decade (Clozapine, Geodon, Seroquel, Risperdal, Zyprexa, Abilify, etc.). It is recommended that sufferers or their carers speak to online support groups to get in touch with others, and to hear about their personal successes and problems with the different medications.

It is also a good idea to read as much as possible regarding the medications available, and talk with a psychiatrist, to identify the medications that may be appropriate.

It should be kept in mind that whilst both the older and newer medications can greatly help a person with schizophrenia, they all have significant side effects that vary according to the individual.

No medication available, unfortunately, constitutes an actual cure for schizophrenia.

A natural treatment for schizophrenia?

While the conclusions drawn range from the positive to the negative, research does suggest that people with schizophrenia may benefit by a reduction in symptoms when they take fish oil capsules that are high in the EPA (a type of Omega-3 fatty acid) form of oil. It is important to be careful about the type of fish oil you are using, as not all fish oils are effective.

Researchers at the University of Sheffield tell us: "What people really need to be looking at is the amount of EPA in the fish oil they are buying.

Our data from previous studies suggests that DHA is of little use in the treatment of schizophrenia, but EPA is the substance that yields the best results. Dosage wise it is suggested that about 2,000 mg/day to 4,000 mg/day (2 to 4 grams/day) should help."

Fish fats, and the oils extracted from them, contain two biologically-active omega 3 fatty acids, DHA, EPA. There are good theoretical reasons why both might be important in the brain. However, with regard to schizophrenia, evidence is accumulating that it is the EPA which is really helpful, whereas DHA may not be beneficial in this context.

The strongest evidence comes from a study at Sheffield University by Dr Malcolm Peet and his colleagues. They did a study in patients with chronic, partially treatment-resistant schizophrenia. These patients continued on their existing medications.

They were then randomised on a double-blind basis to receive either a placebo, or high EPA fish oil from sardines or anchovies, or high DHA fish oil from tuna.

In other words, all the treatments were coded so that neither the patients nor the doctors knew which patient was receiving which treatment until the trial had been completed and the code broken. When the code was broken, the results were very clear.

The placebo patients, as is usual in such experiments, showed a small improvement. The DHA patients also showed a small improvement, but in fact a lesser one than was evident in the placebo group, raising the possibility that DHA may not be helpful.

In contrast, the patients on EPA showed a significant improvement which was comparable to that seen with the newer antipsychotic drugs, yet without the side effects.

Other studies have also shown that the same EPA rich oil as was used in the Sheffield study is very helpful in improving symptoms even in those who have a shorter history of schizophrenia. It therefore seems that the best fish oils to use are those which are high in EPA.

Other Treatment Include:

Diet

Eating a diet that consists of fresh leafy greens, vegetables, probiotic food, omega-3 fatty acids and organic animal protein can go a long way in providing the body great nutrition necessary for great health.

Raw Food

Raw food contains antioxidants that get rid of free radicals and help to repair the cells in the body. Antioxidants are also very important in treating schizophrenia and other mental disorders. Glutathione is the most powerful antioxidant in the body. It's made up of amino acids cysteine, glycine and glutamic acid but cysteine is not made in the body.

That means that glutathione cannot be formed without cysteine. The enzyme involved in the conversion of the above three amino acids into cysteine has been found to be deficient in some individuals with schizophrenia.

You can get cysteine from your diet and its commonly found in garlic, onions, Brussels sprouts, broccoli, red peppers and eggs. It is best to cook animal products but egg yolks can be eaten raw. Try to buy organic produce as much as possible.

Probiotics

Multiple research studies have shown that there is a definite gut brain connection and that probiotics can improve mental health by healing the gut.

Food sensitivities and food allergies combined with genetic susceptibilities have also been implicated in schizophrenia. Removing the offending foods through an elimination diet can be very beneficial.

Omega-3 Fatty Acids

Omega-3 fatty acids are very important for brain function and they are recommended for treating all mental disorders. They exist in three forms: alpha;-linolenic acid (ALA), eicosapentaenoic acid (EPA) and docosahexaenoic acid (DHA).
EPA and DHA can be obtained from algae and fish.

Exercise

Multiple studies have shown that regular exercise can improve mental and emotional disorders including anxiety, depression etc. It also helps to reduce the risk of cancer, diabetes mellitus and heart disease.

Diet, supplements, exercise and other lifestyle changes can be very beneficial for individuals with schizophrenia. Healing the gut and eating a well balanced nutrient-rich diet can go a long way in improving mental health disorders like schizophrenia to the point where symptoms are greatly reduced or even non-existent.

Living and Coping With Schizophrenia

People with schizophrenic symptoms are much more likely to be withdrawn or prefer to be alone most of the time. Some people link them with criminal violence. Despite popular belief, most people with schizophrenia are not violent.

At this time, there is no accurate cure for any of the various types of schizophrenic disorders. In some cases, people with schizophrenia have the ability to live quite independent lives.

It depends upon the condition and severity of their symptoms. With proper medication, most patients are able to control over the disorder.

Numerous researchers estimated that about 28 percent of people suffering from schizophrenia live independently, 20 percent live in group homes, and approximately 25 percent live with their families and relatives.

The sad part is, the remaining 27 percent are either on the streets, living in jails, hospitals or nursing homes.

Almost half of people who are suffering from severe psychiatric illnesses are left untreated. The two main reasons why this happens are the general public's lack of knowledge about where to seek help and the high cost of medication for this illness.

Moreover, some schizophrenics believe in themselves that they have the ability to solve their own problem without applying an effective treatment plan. There is no cure for this type of psychological disorder. Patients must endure a life-long battle and leaving them alone with the disease will not help them.

One thing to remember about schizophrenia is the patient's condition. They need a community that they can trust to help them deal with schizophrenic symptoms.

There are risks of living independently with schizophrenia. Symptoms return when schizophrenics tend to stop taking anti-psychotic drugs because of their side effects which often include restlessness, muscle spasms, blurred vision, over fatigue and weight gain.

Suicide is a serious danger in people with schizophrenia. About 10 percent of people with schizophrenia commit suicide. Young adult males are at highest risk. Also, young adult males have known to commit suicide due to excessive effects of being paranoid especially when they stop their medication. Apart from having a variety of forms and levels, patients with schizophrenia need a proper medication. If this illness is left untreated, the sufferer will not be able to cope with the disorder and get the chance to live independently with the general public.

Subtypes of schizophrenia includes paranoid schizophrenia, trouble performing daily activities, display disturbed movements, residual schizophrenia, and undifferentiated schizophrenia.

Visiting a trusted mental health professional is the most important thing a schizophrenic should do. Regular consultations, taking anti-psychotic drugs on time, and participating in support groups can help patients in controlling their disorder.

Chapter VI

OCD Schizophrenia

Schizophrenia and Obsessive compulsive disorder (OCD) are not alike. Yes, you've read it right. They are two different things but often co-occur with one another. Statistics show that approximately 15 out of 100 people who suffer from OCD also have schizophrenia.

OCD and Schizophrenia: Compared

While these two disorders equally affect both males and females they are often mistaken and interchanged, OCD as schizophrenia or schizophrenia as OCD.

This is because obsessive compulsive disorder and schizophrenia have a lot of things in common and their manifesting signs and symptoms often overlap, same as with the concerned pharmacotherapy and the brain area being affected by both disorder.

It is important to note, however, that many clinical studies show that those who suffer from OCD are less likely to develop schizophrenia, although those with schizophrenia are more likely to develop OCD.

In some cases, symptoms of OCD and schizophrenia may overlap adding to the difficulty of exploring and finding out the clear relationship between these two disorders.

However, one significant manifestation of schizophrenia is the presence of delusions. Delusions are truly false irrational thoughts or beliefs contained by the sufferer even with the presence of strong evidences that suggests those are incorrect.

While obsessions in OCD are usually associated with ideas of contamination, sexual impulses, symmetry or asymmetry, and hoarding things, delusions on the other hand are typically related to illogical thoughts of being a super hero with special powers and ideology associated with persecution wherein the individual with schizophrenia believes that whatever is happening around has always have something to do with him or her.

As it is difficult to diagnose the illness ourselves, it is much advisable to consult experts. Seeking help from a respected psychologist or psychiatrist would be better. They are the ones most eligible in finding natural, traditional, and modern techniques in the course treatment of OCD Schizophrenia.

Chapter VII

Alternative Medications for Schizophrenia

Medication is the most common treatment for this condition, but there are several different alternative and complementary treatments available for those seeking holistic treatment options. Alternative treatments include changes in diet, dietary supplements such as vitamins and herbs, and lifestyle changes.

Seeking Treatment

Schizophrenia is a very serious condition that can lead to harmful behaviors in those suffering from the condition. Because this disorder is serious, seeking treatment from an experienced physician is the first step in the process of recovery.

Treatment with prescription medications allows those with schizophrenia to reduce symptoms while alternative treatments promote overall well-being and mental health. It is generally advised that patients with schizophrenia continue medications until a physician is consulted because there are often serious side effects when medications are suddenly stopped.

Types of Alternative Treatment Available

Alternative treatments for schizophrenia are focused on using dietary supplements, including herbs and vitamins, and making healthy lifestyle changes to encourage mental health. Drugs, such as marijuana, are harmful to patients and may make symptoms of schizophrenia more severe.

Other steps toward health are also important. Reducing and eliminating alcohol and tobacco consumption are both steps toward healing holistically. Other treatments can safely be used with lifestyle changes. Therapy with a licensed therapist, using vitamins and dietary supplements, and

attending group therapies are all options
available.

Therapy and Schizophrenia

Therapy is widely accepted as being
beneficial for anyone suffering from a
mental disorder. Schizophrenia is now
considered as a condition caused by
chemical imbalances in the brain, but
therapy can benefit patients with this
disorder by allowing them space to work
through problems and issues that arise in
their personal life because of the disease.

A psychologist can also provide resources
that patients can use to encourage a healthy
lifestyle. For instance, if rehabilitation
services, such as group home living, is
needed a therapist can provide
recommendations.

Rehabilitation services are an important part
of recovery after beginning a consistent
medication schedule. Rehabilitation can
include vocational and living training to

assist patients in gaining the skills needed to live independently.

Stress management skills are also important for those learning to live independently. Therapy and rehabilitation services are among the most important alternative therapies available for schizophrenic patients today.

Vitamins and Herbs

Modern therapies for schizophrenia can include the use of vitamin supplements or herbs to reduce the symptoms of the disorder and to improve overall health. It is important that patients check with a licensed physician before beginning the use of dietary supplements to ensure the herbal ingredients in supplements won't interact with any prescription medications currently being used.

Some herbs have side effects and interaction precautions that make them unsuitable for use among schizophrenic patients. Vitamins are typically safe if taken according to the instructions on the label, but checking with a primary physician first is recommended.

One of the most common vitamins used in the treatment of schizophrenia is niacin along with Omega 3 fatty acids. This treatment is relatively safe. Some herbal treatments, however, can be dangerous when combined with traditional prescription medications.

For example, St. John's Wort is considered an alternative treatment for schizophrenia but the herb, when combined with medications, can result in lowered blood pressure.

Caution is important when using herbal treatments along with prescription medications. The most successful alternative treatments for schizophrenia are those that can safely and effectively be used in combination with traditional prescription medications.

Advances in medical science have made prescription medications more effective and convenient for use than ever before. Medication, therapy, a healthy lifestyle, and rehabilitation services are the ideal combination of treatments available today.

Why Are Schizophrenia Medication and Treatment Important?

Schizophrenic symptoms usually occur in a person's life during his late teens or throughout his adulthood. According to some researchers, it affects more men than women. There is no cure for life-long condition however it can be treated through proper medication.

Sadly, some people who live with schizophrenia sometimes go off and stop their medication regimen which often allows the symptoms to come and go. The loss of treatment can cause problems which are acutely felt not only by the individual, but by their loved ones and friends as well.
 A successful medication for schizophrenic symptoms, therefore, depends upon a

lifetime treatment of both drug and psychosocial, along with support therapies.

Sufferers of this illness are dealing with a lot of circumstances which are associated schizophrenia. These can be delusions and hallucinations which can have a huge effect in their lives. For example, finding a job will be very difficult for them.

They may have strange feelings and behaviors while interacting with the society. They may have trouble in building social relationships because the symptoms can reduce their coping skills.

In some cases, factors such as poverty, homelessness, and unemployment are frequently associated with this psychological disorder. If the patient is receiving an appropriate treatment and complies with the medication regimen, it is possible for him to live a happy and successful life.

At first, the recovery from the initial symptoms can be very lonely experience. Patients dealing with the disorder for the first time in their lives need all the love and possible support from their family members, relatives, close friends, and their communities.

With such support, strength, and understanding, a schizophrenic can be trained to cope and live with this disorder for his entire life.

A patient can only have this stability by complying with the treatment plan set up based on his condition. Constant communication with their therapist or doctor is important to get more health benefits.

Psychiatric therapy or commonly known as psychotherapy is used as an addition to a good medication plan. It can help maintain the individual on their medication. The process can teach the patients the needed social skills and support their goals in various activities in their community.

Encouraging patients in setting their goals even if they are small ones and guiding them in reaching these goals can often be helpful.

Activities including giving advices, providing assurance, limit setting, and reality testing can be performed with the therapist.

People dealing with schizophrenia often neglect personal hygiene habits. They have trouble in performing ordinary life tasks such as cooking and doing household chores.

It is difficult for these people to communicate with others in the family and even at workplace. A person can possibly regain his confidence to take care of himself and interact with other people and eventually live a fuller life.

A regular psychosocial treatment can provide the patient in preventing relapses or be hospitalized. Psychiatrists or therapists can guide and help patients in living with schizophrenia.

However, a sudden stopping of treatment will lead to a relapse of schizophrenic symptoms and a gradual recovery. The most important thing to remember is to stay on medication regimen provided by your doctor.

How to Reduce Your Chances of Being Diagnosed With Schizophrenia?

Schizophrenia is a type of mental illness that can be very disturbing and can possibly impact a person's quality of life. It can affect the patient's family, friends and other people as well.

As the illness becomes worst, it can keep the patient from functioning in everyday life and may require thorough treatment.

This kind of mental disorder remains an illness that we are still struggling to understand. On the other hand, some scientists believe that people with family members who are suffering from schizophrenia, have a higher risk to get this disorder.

Here is the question, is it possible to prevent the symptoms of schizophrenia? Early prevention is better than cure, there are various ways to help stop schizophrenia and lead a healthy lifestyle. The earlier this psychological disorder is detected and treated, the better the outcome.

In this modern age of medical science, researchers in the field of schizophrenia continue to study to know the causes of this illness along with the possible treatments, such as medication and therapy.

These can control the symptoms and allow the patient to live a quite normal life like the other people do. A relapse prevention plan is critically important in controlling schizophrenic symptoms.

Participating in regular cognitive-behavioral therapy sessions can help a schizophrenic patient in recognizing his delusions. Effective cognitive-behavioral techniques can stop the patient from doing problems which are associated with delusional thinking.
 Numerous schizophrenic patients might stop taking their medicines when they feel better. This can trigger the symptoms to

return. Various medications may give the person side effects that he may not like. However, the patient must take his medication as directed.

There are early danger signs that may indicate a relapse, such as abnormally and easily excitable or exuberant, sleep disturbance, trouble dealing with people, over fatigue, lack of sympathy, pervasive thoughts, compulsive behavior, and delusions or hallucinations.

These signs night indicate that a patient is starting to relapse. As soon as the person recognizes these kinds of symptoms, he should immediately consult his psychiatrist so the relapses of acute episodes of symptoms can be prevented.

Researches in the past decades show that developing schizophrenia is due to genetic factors, early child's development, and environmental stressors which trigger the subtle alterations in the human brain. These brain alterations can make a person susceptible to having schizophrenia.

In addition, environmental stressors that may occur during childhood, adolescence, and young adulthood can damage the brain or reduce the occurrence of neurodevelopmental defects and lessen the risk of schizophrenia.

If a person is a parent and suspected to have a high risk of developing this psychological disorder, there are simple ways to possibly lessen your child's exposure to risk factors.

These steps may take place during the period of pregnancy, prenatal care and early childcare. The first one is to have significant intervals between pregnancies.

Studies show that chances of developing schizophrenia are changing depending on the birth interval. A woman must avoid alcohol, tobacco products, and certain chemicals during pregnancy.

Always remember that it is very important to get enough of the key vitamins for the child's healthy brain development.

How to Cope With Teen Schizophrenia and Its Symptoms?

The most complex of all mental illness is schizophrenia which refers to a chronic and disabling disturbance of the human brain. This psychological disorder is chronic, severe, and brain disease that often occurs to develop between late adolescence and early adulthood.

People dealing with schizophrenic symptoms may have trouble distinguishing reality from fantasy, organizing their thoughts, controlling their emotions, or interacting with others.

Researches show that the disorder affects men and women equally; however, schizophrenic symptoms begin in men earlier than women.

Symptoms usually first appear in men during their late teens or early 20's. Different mistaken beliefs concerning

schizophrenia make it one of the most stigmatized of all mental disorders.
Media may portray misconceptions like people suffering from this disease have split personalities and most of them are violent or tend to harm other people. But of these are not true. Most people with schizophrenia appear aloof and prefer to be left alone.

According to recent researches, one in five teenagers with risk factors developed symptoms of schizophrenia. New imaging studies reveal for the first time patterns of brain development that expand into the teenage years.

The neurological development of young people is very sensitive to aspects of dysfunctional social settings, such as trauma, violence, lack of warmth in personal relationships and lack of sympathy. These factors have all been found for the later progression of schizophrenic symptoms.

Schizophrenia can be confusing and terrifying experience because even people with this mental disorder do not completely understand the nature of their condition. People normally encounter stress during their teenage lives; these pressures can give them the essence of schizophrenia which involves world of fear, confusion and helplessness.

Teens with the disorder may have trouble functioning normally especially when they are interacting with the society.

Schizophrenic symptoms are physically, emotionally and mentally draining for the loved ones of those afflicted. Patients may need possible emotional support from their families, financial assistance, and daily help for medication.

The disorder is physically, emotionally and mentally draining for families of those afflicted. Schizophrenic teens often have difficulty acting normally when they are communicating with general public and may need financial assistance, emotional support and daily help for tasks such as taking medication.

Heredity may play a significant role in having schizophrenia. According to various reports from NARSAD, young people who have a family member with schizophrenic symptoms are 30 percent more likely to develop the mental disorder themselves.

The psychological disorder in teens expresses itself in a different way. It is often difficult to notice and recognize it in the early stages unless evaluated by an expert psychiatrist who specializes in the field of teenage schizophrenia.

Suspected schizophrenic may exhibit behavior changes gradually, over time. In some cases, teens that were once very active in sports and loved hanging out with their friends may start to withdraw and appear aloof.

They may begin to talk about strange events they feel they were a part of, but that never really happened. Some may show childlike behaviors and become dependent upon their parents or guardians.

Challenges to Cope With When Treating Schizophrenia

If your loved one suffers from schizophrenia, he, you and all of your family and friends are facing many challenges to cope with while treating schizophrenia. Here are 5 of the most significant challenges you are going to face during your treatment of schizophrenia:

Maintain a daily routine

If your loved one suffers from schizophrenia, it is going to be a difficult task to get him back to a daily routine. One that would make him occupied and not thinks about his illness all the time.

Being active

When suffering from schizophrenia, your loved one is situated in a place that is being affected by the negative symptoms of schizophrenia and therefore suffers from a lack of energy and motivation to do stuff.

How to ignite him and make him face the reality in an active manner is your real challenge as his loved one.

Being independent

One of the most significant phases of having schizophrenia is lacking the ability to live by you. Therefore how to get him live his life in an independent way with his own protective environment, out of his parents' house is the real challenge.

Having his own income

This is another way to give your loved one the ability to live in an independent way as he should be. When that sufferer has his own job and income and not being dependent on the government support. When having your own money with out giving others a report about what to spend and what not to, is the real meaning of being independent.

Having friends

When people suffer from schizophrenia, they are also suffering from relationships problems such as lack of friend or lack of his own mate. Therefore it is crucial to cause him to get new friends and even to find his own soul mate in order to be able to defeat his schizophrenia disorder.

Chapter VIII

Schizophrenia and Brain Receptors

Scientists from the New Castle University have claimed to have obtained evidences that could prove the probable cause of the abnormalities occurring in the electrical waves of the brains. The research team believes that schizophrenics are deficient in essential brain receptors that control them.

They have conducted a research on rats' where the receptors were diminished with the help of medication to note the changes in wave frequency; the changes did occur and that proved the fact.

Schizophrenia is basically psychiatric disarray which indicates a rare mental disorder with typical characteristics such as perception disorders and/or abnormality in expressing reality.

The disorder commonly manifests abnormalities as acoustic hallucinations, weird delusions or paranoid, disordered speech and thought process with significant dysfunction in their social ass well as occupational aspects.

The symptoms of schizophrenia are likely to onset during adolescence. The diagnosis of this disorder is solely dependent on self-reports provided by the patient of his/her experiences and behavioral conditions; at times others observation might also assist in diagnosis.

Studies have revealed over time that some of the probable contributing factors to schizophrenia could be genetics, neurobiology, early environment, social or some psychological processes. Some drugs; may be recreational or prescribed ones can aggravate the symptoms further.

Recent psychiatric research primarily focuses on the neurobiological factors that could possibly be the real cause of such mental disorder, but no evidences have been found yet.

As there are two many contradictory symptoms of schizophrenia, it is often difficult to conclude whether the diagnosis indicates a single problem or a combination of a couple of distinct symptoms; the debate is still on.

Schizophrenic individuals are likely to have an escalated dopamine activity in the brain's mesolimbic pathway. Antipsychotic medications are the most soughted treatment and are used for subduing the dopamine activity.

Psychotherapy along with social and vocational rehabilitation can also help in this regard. In severe cases where there is a risk for the individual as well as for others - hospitalization is the ultimate way.

Schizophrenia is believed to affect human cognition but, it also has a dramatic impact on an individual's emotions and behavior. Schizophrenics might also have certain comorbid conditions, such as anxiety disorders and severe depression.

Several studies have been carried out to identify the truth of schizophrenia, but no fruitful results have been derived yet. Scientists are still trying their best to look more closely in to the brain functions of people having schizophrenia and the ones who don't - that's the only way of deriving evidence to prove that truth of their suggested theory.

Previously, a difference was derived by researchers related to the "gamma frequency oscillation" - a typical electrical activity pattern found to be different in schizophrenics. The Newcastle research team has aimed to derive real cause of such an alteration.

The research team used Ketamine, a recreational drug for humans that causes hallucinations, a primary symptom of schizophrenia. When this was applied to the brain cells of rats, the frequency of the electrical activities the rat's brain changed dramatically by blocking the brain receptor NMDA.

Chapter VIIII

Smoking Marijuana And The Risks Of Schizophrenia

There is a legitimate and casual link between smoking marijuana and increased rates of psychosis and schizophrenia later in life, and a number of different and independent clinical studies have come to these same conclusions.

If you smoke as a teenager, you are between 2 and 3 times more likely to experience clinical psychosis disorders later in life, and the younger you start smoking, the greater your chance of developing a schizophrenic like disorder.

Secondly, those people who experience a marijuana induced psychotic reaction, (a temporary break with reality while high after smoking marijuana) have about a 50% chance of developing full blown schizophrenia within the following three years.

A causal link to schizophrenia

Researchers have concluded that use is casually linked to the development of schizophrenia, but is not a sole cause, and exists as a component cause amongst many different other factors.

Still, after methodologies which examining the data on marijuana use and schizophrenia, they have determined that if use could be eliminated, there would be an 8% reduction in the cases of later in life schizophrenia, which would be a very significant public health victory.

Schizophrenia remains a poorly understood disease, and the causes that lead to its emergence remain obscured. Researchers suggest that smoking increases the risks of disease expression on people already vulnerable to contract the disease, but who will not necessarily contract the disease.

Marijuana psychosis means a 50% chance of later schizophrenia

This is indicated by those people who do experience a marijuana induced psychotic episode. Marijuana psychosis is not a common occurrence, but does happen and it seems to happen in people already at risk to develop psychosis like disorders later in life.

What seems to be happening though with marijuana induced psychosis is that although the symptoms of the drug induced psychosis will disappear quickly after the effects of the marijuana wear off, it seems to speed up the expression of the schizophrenia by many years.

Patients who do experience a psychosis, on average will present with schizophrenic symptoms years before those people who do not experience a marijuana induced psychosis.

If you do have a marijuana induced psychotic reaction, you are very at risk for later in life schizophrenia, you will probably come down with schizophrenia sooner, and you should take steps to preempt the disease before it emerges. Talk to your doctor about this.

Marijuana causes 8% of all schizophrenia

The vast majority of smokers will not develop schizophrenia as a result of their use, but if we could somehow eliminate the use of the drug, we would see an almost 10% reduction in the prevalence rates of tragic and life changing schizophrenia.

Scientists working on these studies point to the widespread usage of the drug as a problem, and conclude that we as a society are very unlikely to eliminate the usage any time soon. They conclude that for the best public health effects, at risk youth need to be targeted and hopefully deterred from smoking it.

Parents need to keep teens safe from marijuana

For a number of reasons, parents need to be very concerned about use by young teens. It seems as though if parents can keep kids from experimenting with the drug until the age of 18, they spare their children an enormous risk to schizophrenia, and these kids are at a far lower chance to ever develop any real substance abuse problems.

The Complexity of Schizophrenia

In 1911 a Swiss psychiatrist who headed a psychiatric hospital at Burgholzli introduced the term schizophrenia. His work, which was known as "Bleuler's four A's" involved disturbances in affect, association, ambivalence and autism.

Today, the American Psychiatric Association has identified criteria which is used in diagnosis for many disorders including schizophrenia. Three specific categories regarding symptoms must be present and three specific things must be absent before a diagnosis is given.

 A psychiatrist or mental health professional examines the presence and severity of characteristic symptoms which may include delusions, hallucinations, disorganized speech, grossly disorganized or catatonic behaviour or other negatives.

One or more of these is usually apparent for a significant portion of time during a one-month period of time.

Social or occupational dysfunction usually appears in one or more major areas such as work, interpersonal relations or self-care. The performances of children and adolescents may be below expected levels of achievement.

Functioning in adults can clearly be compared between those before onset and those afterwards.

Professionals also study the duration of symptoms and minimally examine a six month period of time before making a diagnosis.

A number of other disorders and conditions must be ruled out. These include schizoaffective, mood disorder, substance abuse, general medical conditions or pervasive developmental disorders.

Yes, the process of diagnosis is complex and to complicate it even further, there are five subtypes of schizophrenia including Paranoid, Catatonic, Disorganized, Undifferentiated, and Residual.

Associated features may include learning problems, hypoactivity, psychosis, euphoric mood, depressed mood, somatic or sexual dysfunction, hyperactivity, guilt or obsession, sexually deviant behaviour, odd/eccentric or suspicious personality, anxious or fearful, dependent, dramatic, erratic or antisocial personality.

Once a diagnosis is made, the professionals involved can help design a treatment plan for the individual. Schizophrenia is not a "curable disease". I know individuals, however, who manage the symptoms and live lives of health, productivity and happiness.

Chapter X

The Specter Of Schizophrenia

What do mathematician John Forbes Nash Jr. and legendary rock star Syd Barrett of the band Pink Floyd have in common?

Both suffered from schizophrenia, a mental disorder that begins between the ages of 15 and 25 and affects about one percent of the population or 51 million people worldwide. Schizophrenia is found in 12 million people in China, 8 million people in India, and over 2 million people in the United States.

Schizophrenia, which is a form of psychosis, is characterized by impairments in the perception or expression of reality. It leads to hallucinations, delusions or disorganization in speech and thinking process.

It usually occurs in young adulthood with approximately 1 percent of the population. Schizophrenia occurs equally in males and females although it typically appears earlier in men with the peak ages of onset being 15-25 years for males and 25-35 years for females.

"People with the condition have a 50 times higher risk of attempting suicide than the general population; the risk of suicide is very serious in people with schizophrenia. Suicide is the No. 1 cause of premature death among people with schizophrenia, with an estimated 10 percent to 13 percent killing themselves and approximately 40 percent attempting suicide at least once (and as much as 60 percent of males attempting suicide)," according to Schizophrenia.Com, a non-profit web community that provides information, support, and education to people with schizophrenia.

The symptoms of schizophrenia fall into three categories: positive, negative or cognitive. Positive symptoms include hallucinations, delusions, and disorders of movement.

Patients may see, hear, smell or feel something that normal people don't. They often hear voices that comment on their behavior, order them to do things, or warn them of impending danger.

They see people or objects that aren't there, and smell odors that no one else detects. Delusions take the form of false beliefs where patients think that they are famous or people are plotting against them or spying on them.

One famous victim of schizophrenia was the Nobel Laureate mathematician John Forbes Nash Jr. who was portrayed by Russell Crowe in the critically-acclaimed film, "A Beautiful Mind." The story tells of Nash's early days at Princeton University where he meets his roommate Charles and his niece Marcee.

Nash is later approached by Department of Defense agent William Parcher to help the Pentagon decipher secret messages to thwart a Soviet plot. At the end of the movie, we learn that all three people never existed and are products of Nash's troubled mind.

Syd Barrett, a founding member of the rock band Pink Floyd was a brilliant musician whose musical career was cut short by schizophrenia. His first album influenced generations of musicians and made him a superstar. As the disease progressed, however, Barrett suffered from weird thoughts, odd behavior, bizarre actions, disorganized thinking, and catatonia. He withdrew from public view at the age of 28 and stayed home until his death at age 60.

Chapter XI

Bipolar Disorder And Schizophrenia - Various Differences Explained

Medical professionals, for years, were under the assumption that schizophrenia and bipolar were two diseases with very comparable symptoms. German psychiatrist Eric Kraepelin said that the illnesses were very different mental disorders. Separation of the two diseases still exists even today thanks to Kraepelin.

People need to understand that these two diseases are very hard to distinguish from one another because they do have the same symptoms and signs which makes it difficult for psychiatrists not to make mistakes in diagnosis.

However, brain specialists and some psychiatrists have narrowed down the signs of both bipolar disorder and schizophrenia

and are able to form a base for their
diagnosis.

Bipolar vs Schizophrenia

Bipolar people can have schizophrenia-like
hallucinations or delusions. The difference
between the two though is that bipolar in its
form is constant or rather chronic. In
schizophrenia, there are signs of depressive
and manic episodes like the ones in found in
bipolar disorder.

Due to their similarities, it would be difficult
for a family member or non-medical
professional make the distinction between
the two. There have been cases where some
psychiatrists have made mistakes as well.
There are also cases where severe
schizophrenia have resembled severe cases
of the highs and lows of bipolar disorder.

Researchers have found that genetics play a
major factor for both diseases. This fact
means medical professionals can find a
considerable difference between the two by
studying patient's genetics.

Bipolar vs Schizophrenia - Treatments for Mental Illnesses

Available today are treatments for both illnesses that can successfully help in managing bipolar disorder and schizophrenia. Psychotherapy along with medications that can change the chemistry of the brain go a long way in managing the illnesses.

The medicines along with talk therapy sessions help to stabilize the functions in the brain thus lessening the signs and symptoms effects.

Note: Remember that since bipolar disorder and schizophrenia are very close together in the way they present themselves, it is not hard for even a medical professional to mistake them. Medicines given for one when the patient has the other disease will not work.

This is when the patient would need to speak with the physician about the issue. If he or she is unable to speak about it, a trusting relative should.

One of the more popular drugs given to schizophrenia patients is Clorazil. It designed especially for schizophrenia and should never be given to bipolar patients. It is intended for them to get their brain functions under control.

Those who suffer from bipolar disorder are often prescribed Lithium which is a very effective drug that keeps manic episodes from recurrence. For those who have fast cycling bipolar illness, specialist like to give Valproic acid. This can be good for regular cycling bipolar too.

It is important that a person suffering from either these two diseases or a trusted friend or relative choose a doctor that can be entrusted to care for the patient or loved one. They must be well-recognized in the field of mental illnesses. By choosing the right doctor, the patient will get the right form of treatment necessary for their recovery and medications to help it along.

Schizophrenia and bipolar should be diagnosed as early as possible for the treatment to be more valuable.

Since these two mental diseases can cripple your life and make you an "unproductive" member of society, it is best to get treated as soon as you or someone else suspects something. If not, it will worsen over time and greatly affect how you live, work, and relate to friends, family and the outside world.

Leading a Healthy Life With Schizophrenia

Coping with schizophrenia is not just hard for the sufferer, but can also be difficult for his family members and loved ones as well. Although schizophrenia can be a complicated and contradictory disorder, always keep in mind that living with this psychological disorder is possible for everyone involved.

Even if you have diagnosed schizophrenia, there are various ways to return and live a normal life.

The key to living a healthy life despite of this mental illness lies in a combination of factors: finding the right medical regimen or interventions, developing the right attitude, and staying positive and consistent.

At first, if a family member or friend is suffering from the disorder, it is important to remember that they are not accountable for causing it, and you cannot solve or cure it for them.

Also, another important thing to keep in mind is that even though you have the best intentions for them, the symptoms might actually get worse from time to time.

It is usually as difficult for the patient to accept the illness as it is for the people around them. For that reason, acceptance and patience are ideal, even though they might not always be possible to exist.

Understanding about the mental disorder is very important, and trying to separate the person from his disorder might help out as far as patience and acceptance goes.

Furthermore, reasoning with a delusion will not make it leave. The person with schizophrenic symptoms might on some level know that the thing that they feel is a delusion, or they might not. Delusions, the events, voices, or hallucinations appear to be very real for the sufferers; therefore, being calm during an outburst is important.

Avoid trying to do anything to agitate the situation. However, if the individual threatens to do something that can harm you or themselves, then it is important to call for help.

The need to overcome schizophrenic symptoms is very critical given the average statistics of individuals diagnosed with this mental illness.

According to mental health experts, there are approximately 2.5 million people suffering from the disorder. The good news is that 10 to 20 percent of these figures were able to achieve the successful recovery from the condition.

In fact, there are numerous famous personalities who became successful in their respective fields in spite of being previously diagnosed with the disorder. These famous people include author Jack Kerouac, Syd Barrett (Pink Floyd guitarist), and the Nobel Prize recipient John Nash.

Identifying the common problems that hinder you towards the successful treatment is a key method to achieve a successful recovery. These may include positive and negative symptoms, and the possibility of developing side effects, especially with antipsychotic drugs or medications. Relying solely on your medication regimen is not enough, a successful recovery can happen with a combination of counseling, antipsychotic drugs, therapy, and other treatment procedures.

To lead a healthy life, it is very important to find a treatment that also addresses the negative symptoms of this illness.

Why Knowing About Schizophrenia is Important

The scary thing about schizophrenia is that sufferers may be so confused by the symptoms that they are unable to tell what is real and what is fantasy.

For instance, when serial killer David Berkowitz saw black dogs barking out orders to kill, he believed they were actually there.

Many schizophrenics keep their voices and thoughts to themselves, for fear of being labeled "crazy." Another schizophrenic, Janice Jordan, mentioned being unable to tell her counselors about a delusional figure known as "The Controller" who barked orders at her during psychotic episodes.

The more patients learn about the illness and its many effects, the better equipped they are to handle the symptoms. Unfortunately, taking life-long medication is also a realistic assumption on the road to recovery.

Schizophrenia research reports some interesting findings. For instance, the mental illness is largely caused by a neuro-chemical imbalance of Dopamine, Seratonin and Norepenephrine.

In a normal brain, the frontal lobe increases its blood flow and the "listening" part of the brain diminishes. PET scans reveal that in a schizophrenic brain, the frontal lobe is active but the "listening" part remains just as active.

The sensory overload usually causes a hallucination. People who are born with it generally have irregular brain cell patterns. Drugs and stress do not cause schizophrenia, but they can certainly exacerbate the symptoms.

In some cases, family members who understand very little can agitate the symptoms by using an accusing tone of voice or reacting angrily to the sufferer.

Family members who know about schizophrenia can learn to recognize symptoms of an acute attack: a change in personality, social withdrawal, sleeplessness, agitation, using words that do not make sense and seeing things that aren't there. It is important to create an environment that facilitates recovery.

Keeping peace and serenity at home, helping the schizophrenic set realistic goals, sharing tasks, gradually increasing independence and encouraging new hobbies can all provide schizophrenia support.

There are many misperceptions about schizophrenia. One is that schizophrenia is the same as multiple personality disorder (MPD), which is simply not true. MPD is often characterized by two or more separate and distinct "personalities" which sometimes go by different names, display different mannerisms and have entire lists of unique likes and dislikes.

By contrast, schizophrenics exhibit different behavior, as well as suffer delusions and hallucinations. However, they maintain a basic sense of self, afflicted by mood swings and fragmented thinking. Another misperception is that sufferers are violent by nature.

Chapter XII

Computer-Based Therapy Can Help Treat Patients of Schizophrenia

Schizophrenia is not as common as other mental disorders like anxiety or depression, but the symptoms can be quite disabling. The person afflicted with the condition may lose touch with reality and can think, act and behave differently.

A recent research suggested that a computer-based approach can be effective in helping people battling schizophrenia.

The researchers found that on interacting with a computer avatar, which represents their hallucinations, patients can feel an improvement in the symptoms.

The results of avatar therapy were compared with that of supportive counseling and it was found that the former was effective in reducing auditory hallucinations after a 12-week follow-up.

The study, published in the journal The Lancet Psychiatry in November 2017, comprised 150 participants who were struggling with schizophrenia for the past two decades and were experiencing distressing auditory hallucinations continuously for over a year.

Half of the study population was provided with avatar therapy and the remaining was given supportive counseling. All the participants continued taking their antipsychotic medications alongside the therapies.

Avatar therapy versus supportive counseling

Before starting the avatar therapy, the participants worked with the therapists to create their avatars or the computer simulation of the voice which they wanted to tame with features like how it looked and what it said.

The avatar sessions lasted for about 50 minutes each, over a period of six weeks. The sessions comprised a three-way dialogue between the patient, therapist and avatar (voiced by the therapist).

Every session had a set target and included a face-to-face interaction, lasting for around 10-15 minutes between the patient and his or her avatar.

During these one-on-one interactions, patients learned the art of standing up to those distressing voices and clearing any misconceptions. This led to a better control of the situation and a shift in power from the avatar to the patient.

Eventually, the avatar realized patient's strengths, positive qualities, higher control and greater power in the relationship. Each session was recorded and handed over to the patient to listen to when they heard the voices again.

The supportive counseling also comprised the same number of sessions and tried helping patients by suggesting ways of improving their overall quality of life. The sessions ended by recording a positive message.

After a period of 12 weeks, the patients who took avatar therapy reported a marked alleviation in the disturbing symptoms and power of the voices they often heard. They fared better than their counterparts who were offered supportive counseling.

Ways to Release From the Fixation of Not Being Able With Schizophrenia

Be assertive

Sufferers of schizophrenia disorder should act in an assertive way. They should claim things for themselves that otherwise will not be given to them due to their schizophrenia. They should stand up for their right to be treated as normal as possible.

Find a job

In order to be independent and earn your
own money without being supported by the
government, people who suffer from
schizophrenia should find a job that both
keep them occupied during most of the day
and therefore not thinking only about their
illness, and earn a decent living from it.

Find a mate

One of the most important polls in life is
your partner to life, your boy or girl friend,
or your sole mate. A partner in life helps
very much to deal with the daily lives and
support you in everything you do. He or she
is also the person to talk and share with
almost about anything.

Do exercise

Keeping your physical body healthy at all
times is a key to have a healthy mind.
Exercising does not refer to intensive
workouts. You can do simple exercises by

going out of the house every morning and spend 45 minutes walking or jogging, or participating in physical activities that make your body move.

Regular exercise can give you various benefits such as staying in shape, reducing the level of bad cholesterol, and minimizing one's blood pressure. Moreover, it makes you feel good about yourself, which is very important in coping with the mental disorder.

Defining goals

One of the most important ways to release sufferers from their fixation is by determine goals in life and going to reach them. It also helps them to show themselves that they are capable of doing stuff and get things that others think they can't.

Promote Balance in Life

In a person's life, balance is very important. For instance, if you wanted to control the schizophrenic symptoms, try to achieve balance in whatever you do. Too much of something is not good.

Conclusion

You do not have to let schizophrenia change the way you live. This book was written to inspire you and to educate you on how to deal with a loved one with schizophrenia. Stand by their side at all times and show them love and understanding. With proper nourishment of the mind, this awful disorder can be managed under control.